Rivers in My Veins

Saint Julian Press

Poetry

Praise for — *Rivers in My Veins*

With calm elegance, precise language, and the spirit of the Pacific Northwest, Kara Briggs sings her people onto the page. *Rivers in My Veins* is both protest and celebration, a reminder to readers that the Sauk-Suiattle, Wenatchee, Chelan, Entiat, and Skagit peoples are still harvesting, fishing, and remembering. Land we live on land, she writes, calling us to embrace our kinship with the earth.

—Deborah Taffa
Whiskey Tender

Rivers in My Veins is a work of lyric courage that celebrates the interconnectivity of the earth and her people while confronting, through unflinching investigative addresses, the false settler-colonial narratives and power structures within these narrative's problematic etymologies and extractive practices. Kara Briggs' tenacious spirit and fierce love of the lands, waters, and stories of her Coast Salish people makes *Rivers in My Veins* a powerful debut collection that will become a vital contribution to our shared world's literary—and deeply alive—landscapes.

—Jennifer Elise Foerster
Editor – *When the Light of the World Was Subdued*
Our Songs Came Through: A Norton Anthology of Native Nations Poetry

With a journalist's eye for unflinching truth, Kara Briggs's *Rivers in My Veins* assembles precise language, lyric verse and innovative form to produce a finely wrought blend of Native perspective poetry. Briggs compels the reader to hold onto familiar narratives of landscape and family while learning more layers of story. At the heart of this collection, a drum of knowledge beats, aiming at nothing less than uplifting the experience of American Indians who are every bit as intellectual and human as the readers of this book. I have known Kara Briggs for many years waiting for this collection to come to light. Now we will be better as a nation for reading *Rivers in My Veins*.

—Suzan Shown Harjo
Presidential Medal of Freedom Recipient
Editor – *Nation to Nation: Treaties Between*
the United States and American Indian Nations

In groundbreaking forms and language that speak directly to her ancestors, elders, and future generations, Kara Briggs amplifies the legacy of her Sauk-Suiattle and Yakama peoples and of Native American poets writing before her to place her family and tribal histories outside of the parenthesis forever. Reading *Rivers in My Veins* remains a journey in poetry that I will carry in my veins forever. I am grateful; I am humbled, but most importantly, I am eager for the conversations that Briggs' debut river of poetry will provoke in American letters.

—Sandra Yannone
The Glass Studio and *Boats for Women*

The poems in Kara Briggs's debut, *Rivers in My Veins*, awe with their gorgeous imagery and their unparalleled wisdom. They will make you cry, cause you to seethe with anger, and comfort you with their testimony of resilience. Deeply embedded in the culture of the Coast Salish and Interior Salish peoples, *Rivers in My Veins* is spiritual, ascendant, and damning. In some poems, Briggs pierces the reader by bringing home the personal toll caused by devastating colonial acts like the flooding of Celilo Falls, while in others she insightfully meditates on the meanings of fraught terms like "sovereignty" and "apology." The book moves from breathless love poems such as "Ancestor Moon," where the speaker is "turned to mist," to poignant explorations of the tragedy of in-fighting within the speaker's Tribal community. The strikingly lyrical poems in *Rivers in My Veins* beguile with their beauty and at the same time teach you how to live.

—Ann Tweedy
The Body's Alphabet and *A Registry of Survival*

Rivers in My Veins

Poems

by

Kara Briggs

SAINT JULIAN PRESS
HOUSTON

Published by
SAINT JULIAN PRESS, Inc.
2053 Cortlandt, Suite 200
Houston, Texas 77008

www.saintjulianpress.com

Paperback ISBN-13: 978-1-955194-35-8
eBook EPUB ISBN-13: 978-1-955194-36-5
Library of Congress Control Number: 2024939387

Cover Art Credit: Ramon Shiloh – Mvskoke/Cherokee/Filipino/African American
Author Photo Credit: Mel Ponder Photography

P r e f a c e

Rivers in My Veins will be called Indigenous or Native American poetry, and if it all goes well it will be shelved in Native American sections of bookstores, taught in Native American Studies courses, reviewed as such in publications. And this will be correct in that the author is a Native American enrolled in a tribe called Sauk-Suiattle from the foothills of the North Cascade Mountains. Many of the characters related through these poems are also Native Americans, as are the landscapes and rivers. Not to belabor the point, these were the themes intended for this, her first collection of poetry, developed while the author attended the Master of Fine Arts Creative Writing program at the Institute of American Indian Arts (IAIA).

Yet the risk of saying this is to pigeonhole the poet, to say this is all she knows, this is her whole experience. And in that, to miss the lyricism born not only in the oral history and social dances of her tribes, but also in her deep reading of 20th Century American poetry, in her decades as a journalist covering the American West for leading newspapers, the influence of W.S. Merwin, of Dick Hugo, of Carolyn Kizer, of Seamus Heaney, of Eavan Bolan, of the journalist Joseph Boyce, the poet, journalist and Presidential Medal of Freedom recipient Suzan Shown Harjo. And to miss the author's deep love of jazz, especially the phrasing of the vocalist Carmen McRae, the powwow high notes of jazz artist Mildred Bailey, Coeur d'Alene Tribe.

This journey into poetry began during a conversation she had as an undergrad at Whitworth College in Spokane, Wash., with poet Phillip Levine who told her that although she was a Native American woman, as an English language poet she was a responsible for an understanding of the canon of English language poetry. She took that to heart reading a wide range of authors and genres for many years before coming to IAIA in the midst of the Covid 19 pandemic shutdown.

Any book with the word veins in its title is going to challenge readers to open their thinking, to sit with uncomfortable ideas, to sound out words in Native languages for perhaps the first time, as a child encountering words for the first time. Just as the lyrical words and forms nourish the entirety of the lyrical experience in the way river water flows from mountains, this book requires the reader to see with a new lens.

The poem "Acknowledgement Two" from this collection received the 2024 James Welch Prize for Indigenous Poetry from Poetry Northwest. The late Blackfeet novelist James Welch who also wrote poetry is an inspirational figure to tribal and other writers in the Northwest.

"Acknowledgement Two" is both lyric and documentary poetry, telling the stories of the author's late uncle Alvin Settler, Yakama Nation, and other tribal fishers from the Columbia River, who witnessed the inundation of the culturally important Celilo Falls behind a federal dam project, who witnessed and survived the period of suppression of their treaty right to fish only decades later to watch the decline of salmon runs because of federal management of the river.

Other forms used include sonnet (both Italian and Shakespearian), sestina (Italian), pantoum (Malaysian), riddle (Old English), villanelle (French) and the haibun and haiku (Japanese).

Briggs has said that using form poetry is part of her writing practice. It helps her shape poems even if the form is not evident until the final version is drafted. She also views form poetry as a way of connecting the reader to unknown or challenging stories.

As an innovator, the author devised her own forms and rhythms studying the social songs of Northwest Tribes. The poem "Swan Dance" is based on one of these social dances, with roots thousands of years old among the tribes of the mid-Columbia River. The series of haiku inspired poems titled "Passings" explores poems that combine the brevity of this Japanese form with cultural numbers and imagery from the Coast Salish tribes. The series "Sauk-Suiattle Struggles" is inspired by Simon Ortiz's "Sand Creek Massacre" and its take on history viewed from contemporary Native peoples' viewpoints.

Rivers in My Veins is the first collection of poetry produced by an experienced and gifted writer capable of telling complex stories, in many styles, using lyrical and powerful language to connect the reader to a world unfamiliar. *Rivers in My Veins* gives voice to stories of the past to move into the future and reconnect to the lands and waters.

FOR NORMA JOSEPH

CHAIRWOMAN OF THE SAUK-SUIATTLE INDIAN TRIBE

CONTENTS

Weaving with my Grandmothers   1

By the Creekside   2

Girl in the Lake   3

Etymology /əkˈnäləjmənt/   4

Acknowledgement One   5

Acknowledgement Two   6

Acknowledgement Three   7

Acknowledgement Four   8

Acknowledgement Five   9

Desloot's Wápaas   10

Etymology /ˈsäv(ə)rən(t)e/, ˈ/Sävərn(t)e/   12

Does Jackson Sundown Yet Ride?   13

Winter Light   15

The Mountains, Our Relations   16

Ancestor Moon   18

Sauk-Suiattle Life   19

Etymology /inˈdigˈeˈnous/in-di-jə-nəs/   20

Swan Dancers   21

Nch'i-Wana   22

PDX Urban Indian Life   23

A Dream of Language   24

Photographer Edward Curtis' Subjects in Three Parts   25

    One: The Women   25

    Two: Chief Joseph   26

    Three: 21st Century Indians   27

Ancestor Gold   28

Etymology /əˈpäləjē/   29

Siskiyou Pass   30

Jazz Parents   32

Sudden Death   35

Taking My Place   37

When First We Met   38

Industrial River   39

Etymology | jen-uh-sahyd   40

Declaring Our Indigene   41

Bird Life   42

Passage   43

Words   44

Sauk-Suiattle Struggles   46

Celilo   59

Rivers in My Veins

Weaving with my Grandmothers

my hands fly around a wooden loom, wrapping dyed yarn for warp
my teacher says you've done this before, I answer no
my teacher admires the movement of my hands, the tightness of fiber
to wood I say I must have seen this on TV, my teacher says no
my hands take the weft, alternating hands and yarns, one white, one
red my teacher calls this weaving with both hands flying
each hand with its own ball of yarn
my teacher calls this butterfly wings
I say the only butterflies are in my stomach, my teacher says no
weft rounds warp
pull tight, my teacher says, your grandmother
must have been a weaver
I say no, my grandmother, a nurse, didn't have the time
my teacher says all our grandmothers' hands move in ours
I stop weaving, I say yes, a grandmother of mine was a weaver

my teacher says this is how we remember

yarn, hands, motion

By the Creekside

For Carolyn Kizer

all numbers have been changed

if we had come of age together, gentle poet
we could have shared, not the cotillion
    but walks on creek bed

with found sticks we'd loosen blue-green pebbles
while tiny schools of trout race past, tickling
    our submerged feet

much can be learned from reading a creek bed
aquatic repositories, await interpretation
under layers of sediment,
    footprints of ancestors,
      not thieves as you suppose

we are not so different, you and I
poet, writer, judge
interpreter of the signs
of our suburban childhoods
    separated by decades
 burnished by the same hot sun

whispers from shadows in our bedrooms
tell stories that we as children could not bear
shadows scare us
    shadows are not the lions
 you imagine, but white-tailed deer
      leaping out window into stars

we hold quiet agreement on the power of animals
 when our prayers are said, we are still
    holding hands, skating down that frozen creek
    until we can't feel our fingers or toes
we laugh all the way home
      to hot cocoa by the fire

Girl in the Lake

For Janice Gould

The Acoustic Research Detachment opened in World War II on Lake Pend Oreille, taking advantage of the 1,150-foot-deep channel at Bayview, Idaho. Testing echolocation that was used to unmask Nazi U-boats in the Atlantic, little was remembered about the first time this little piece of nowhere in particular changed history. In prehistoric time, ice dams atop these basalt cliffs burst releasing what would be called the Missoula Flood. In modern times the only Nazis in North Idaho are the homegrown kind. A Native woman with black sons couldn't get hired to run the now historic Acoustic Research Detachment in 2020 because of her sons' race. Mountain goats atop lava rock cliffs stand in silent witness all along. I grew up 20 minutes from there. Little is remembered of the Indian girl who lived at the Acoustic Research Detachment with her father in the 1950s, and who grew up to be the Round Valley poet named Janice Gould.

water, a girl steps
on sunspots making a path
on white capped waves

girl gathers words in
her hem to write on blue rock
canyon walls her home

weightless it seems a
mountain goat can carry her
where she needs to go

girl slips into blue
green water, breathing carries
sound to underwater black

broken black by knife
of white light, green blade
of verse never faulter girl

Etymology /əkˈnäləjmənt/

I come to realize

what took place

the ancient k-n

ack, I cough

I know, am known, now know

what needs to be said

a stem called ment

I act, I take action

on all that was taken

on all that was kept

a ledge

to lie, to lay

to lay for, to lay low, to lay an egg

I lay down on a cedar plank

on this curving earth, saltwater swirling

a spear

keeping account, awaiting revenge

Acknowledgement One

Across two continents and one island acknowledgement of the land
that once belonged to Indigenous peoples is on trend. Like pledges
or prayers, said with slight variance in sincerity at public meetings,
classrooms, theatres in the United States, Canada, Australia, New
Zealand; these imagine a place where words can heal, where the
perished can hear, where the land is virgin, devoid of people. Land
as real estate, to be transferred by will or sale, we acknowledge this
transaction. The nations that came before and those that still
remain are unnamed, other than in their words that name land.
Attorneys for jurisdictions in state governments assure wobbly
public officials that acknowledgements have no legal standing, no
real meaning despite the decorum, the emotive expression that the
children of immigrants deploy when reading.

land we live on land we own
land rights we reserved on paper
homelands landscapes greenspaces
council fires once burned
on land now burning
land traditional, land ancestral, land stolen
land violently stolen
subject to treaty, not subject to treaty
land without record
land aboriginal
we hunted deer, they hunted us like deer
the soldiers triggered by PTSD or opium
said in journals that my uncles looked like deer

Erase the land, will the people still exist?
Erase the people, you can take the land.

Acknowledgement Two

America is my home and my hammer, and it's hammering me, uncle says as he plants his feet on scaffold, a round net big enough to catch the moon or a salmon leaping up Celilo Falls, quicksilver, shimmering blinding uncle's eyes. Muscles in uncle's arm still flex and bulge even if only triggered by remembering the river that isn't, the falls that aren't, the run that's gone, the fish that leaped into the night sky when the river ran backwards that day the Dalles Dam concrete walls slammed shut. Rivers flow to ocean, not backwards, not settled into this series of reservoirs. The people wept as generations of salmon hammered their heads on the cement wall of that damn dam. Uncle bought a speed boat, took to casting lines and later gill nets on a flat-surfaced reservoir. What had become of the Big River, Nch'i Wána and its ballet of salmon no longer leaping up waterfalls while uncle perched above waiting.

Uncle holds a well-thumbed yellow book on Oregon's revised fishing codes, the dog-eared page where it said except for Indian fishers. Uncle dug out a foot hold in the law where an Indian fisher could build a life. Uncle bought land on the riverbank, a pretty hillside where hazelnut trees still grow, where the sun baked dry the salmon, where his wife baked bread in a wood-fired oven, where he and she grew old, their radical days recorded in documentaries, in interviews, in legal decisions won, lost. They are minor celebrities now, known to urban dwellers longing for old style protests, misinterpreting radical for what was just survival, and what wasn't all that romantic because the bullets were real, the arrests were targeted, the divorces were inevitable. Dying in Toppenish elder housing where he lived with his second wife, uncle stretched out his arms like an Old Testament prophet giving a blessing, told me to carry this story into a future he won't live to see, we might not live to see, salmon might not live to see, the Big River might not even live to see.

Acknowledgement Three

As a child my grandmother spoke three languages fluently.

She stood among adults translating.

She knew the names of all the medicine plants and how high in the mountains they grew.

She could recite the family tree from memory.

Sometimes, because she was still a child, she played poly-linguistics tricks on her parents, who laughed and worried what world would this child grow up into.

By today's standard this child would be gifted and talented.

Then she was sent to St. George's boarding school more than 100 miles and across one major mountain range from her home.

With every year she was at school her words slipped away, her playfulness slipped away, her recollection slipped away. Or she hid it like someone in a witness protection program.

When I was a child and my grandmother was an old woman, we held hands and remembered what we couldn't remember.

We cried for languages we no longer knew, names beyond memory, relationships broken on the sharp chards of time.

What stayed with her was the smell of plant medicine. She could smell it from afar and say what that plant would heal.

What stayed with her were the dreams where she heard people talking in her languages and understood them as long as she was asleep.

What stayed was our hands in each other's hands, knowing even what we couldn't remember.

Acknowledgement Four

(Optional reader participation: Use your own expressions, like a silent-film star to act out impatience, frustration and outrage where the blank lines occur.)

Once there were houses on the Sauk and Suiattle allotments in the foothills North Cascades. Once there were gardens. Once there were drying sheds for salmon. Once in the 1960s all this was here.

Then the U.S. Forest Service gave them 20 minutes to clear out, 20 minutes to pack up life, 20 minutes that you didn't have if you weren't at home on that day in the 1960s. Then the U.S. Forest Service set fire to each house and shed, one after another, ready or not.

That day the U.S. Forest Service committed genocide to the tune of $___ per allotment, adjusted for inflation to the tune of $_____.

What my Aunt Norma said when she was the tribal chair is this: the bill is due, overdue, owed in full now.

What the U.S. Forest Service said was

_____.

What the U.S. Congress said was

_____.

What the White House said was

_____.

What I want to know is did the regalia of generation dance in those fires that day?
Did the rattle shake one last time?
Did Great Uncle's moccasins take to the floor for a last dance?
Did Great Aunt's basket let loose a whistle of the tune she sang when she weaved late into the night?
Did the salmon drying on the rack take a last leap into the atmospheric river of the sky?
And what I really want to know is when is the U.S. going to pay our bill?

Acknowledgement Five

In the summer when the earth pulls down the night like a blanket, I stand in warmth imparted from the sun into my paved driveway, and gaze skyward in the dark. I see the Milky Way and feel as if it is just beyond my reach.

Luminous clouds and smoke form a lizard in my sight, like those I witness lying still in the midday sun, now lying amid the night sky.

The stars so far away that they cannot be seen individually, like my ancestors from Sauk, Entiat, Chelan, Wenatchee, who go so far back in time that I cannot distinguish them all standing on these same mountains looking at these same stars.

We make our own meaning of these stars and the meteors that shoot toward our sky. We understand our own sky in our own terms, the familiar first star, the blue and red stars I see as cornflowers and poppies in a field, when once I only saw black and white.

The history of light is carried in these stars. The light in my eyes is thousands of years old. I am a witness to the history of this galaxy, whose light we depend upon to live on earth, light that shines even when I turn off my electricity.

The earth and stars are in permanent motion, like my body is in a permanent movement as long as I am alive. Standing in my driveway in the dark, I feel as if I could stand still forever looking skyward, but it is an illusion like the light in my eyes.

The earth pulls down the night's star quilt, pulls down light that may not exist even now as I stand here. I exist between the stars out of my reach and the continual weight of gravity binding me to earth.

Desloot's Wápaas

I met Desloot

walking over a mountain

wenatchi river hold

a revere

snow isn't cold, sun isn't warm

a memory

grandmother generations

my feet always in her steps

     5000 feet where the huckleberry thrive

     DNA cedar and huckleberry

held in our wápaas

traced in our bodies

     purple berry juice stains our lips

       our relative bear

         already picking

  peace between us

Desloot opens her mouth

a whisper

I can understand

the roundness of her body

fingers stained and stubby

                 callused from weaving root

      as mine are callused

from holding a pen

wind begins to talk

about rivers flowing west

salt air blows east

we are a counter current

salt in our blood gives evidence

we are salmon in icicle creek

we find our way

           home on this mountain

Etymology /ˈsäv(ə)rən(t)ē/,ˈ/sävərn(t)ē/

superior

pre-eminent authority

vulgar Latin for

powerful chief

any gender

extremely potent

like chemotherapy

will kill or save

sounding so close, benign or malign

it could go either way, every cancer survivor knows

a magnum of champagne

and I won't remember the battle

or a gold coin or

a butterfly I cannot catch

Does Jackson Sundown Yet Ride?

For Bobbie Connor

comet golden on a moonless night
boy's view unobscured on a barren hill
a herd of ponies, Indian ponies, his right
he listens for musket fire

until sunrise, then rides herd north
because he knows his people depend upon him

Jackson Sundown took to rodeo
in old age, whirlwind
on bucking horse, he hung on
like a horsefly they said,
clung on that comet
riding for the stars, until the horse
gave out, walked out
or swan-dived in the dirt

in that 70 seconds while all
the world watched his white hat fly
off, his white chaps the only thing
visible between his brown
skin and that chestnut gelding
in those seconds, did he recall
the war for Wallowa
Joseph and White Bird
the boy he was driving the herd to find
Sitting Bull's Band north
of the border, north of surrender

Jackson Sundown's fame
came at age 49 when he signed
to compete in the Pendleton Round Up
a slender man, pure muscle
he captivated crowds, won the purse

had his picture taken
with the city fathers, smiled at cameras
some say he could ride that way
because he had the horsefly spirit
some say he was born on horseback
some say he died on horseback

some say it was just the damn flu

Winter Light

Haboo

in fire light

whispered in breath

Haboo

in the bloodstream

Haboo

spoken

to cedar

contained in winter light

put away in the first light of spring

The Mountains, Our Relations

as told by Norma Joseph

listen to me, I have something to say

the usually soft-spoken matriarch walks

to the center of the floor

somehow, we can all hear her soft voice

speaking as she is beginning a conversation:

my grandfather was the most handsome man

Sobaliali was his name

it was a name so old that no one knew its meaning

it was said the creator told it to the ancient ones

Sobaliali was dressed all in white

the day a beautiful woman from the east

caught his eye with her white fur cape

her hair woven with beads and shells

her name was Ćaqʷubəʔ, she sparkled in the sun

they married

and were very happy for a time

then one day a woman with a headband of flowers

her dress sewn from rainbow

arrived from the west

as Sobaliali and Hədalgʷəs lingered with their heads close

Ċaqʷubəʔ scratched the face of Hədalgʷəs

a fight began, the ground rumbled

as their feet stomped

the low hills let go mud sending it

cascading into valleys

Sobaliali, worried for Ċaqʷubəʔ, placed her behind him

out of Hə›dalgʷəs reach

to this day you can see the scratches on the face of Hədalgʷəs

and Ċəqʷubʷəʔ always waiting for Sobaliali to return home

as my matriarch ends her story, her eyes

see us marveling at the mountains

our ancestors

who stand all around us

bearing witness

Ancestor Moon

and yet the smell of him like a wild beast
perfume of pine mountain soil he must
have heard my spirit call not him my quest
my purpose my guide I am turned to mist
wild valerian in my hair I am obsessed
I run, black hair behind turns to dust
he answers, a breathing man, not ghost
petroglyph memory I align to night
darkness him alone I have no might
a dream I once heard, tell me, is it right
that I, a lonely searcher with no fight
blackberry moon, beguiling and bright

chiefly my heart I say when wedded I
return, he is mine, I his, this I cry

Sauk-Suiattle Life

seaweed, salmon, eels
cook in sandy fire pits
boiling salt water

hauled salt water
far inland, evaporate
all but precious salt

red flash, Skykomish
River salmon, journey home
spawn generations

Etymology /in·dig·e·nous/in-di-jə-nəs/

to indu

to endow

to beget, begotten

forgotten birthed

dug up anyway

to dig it up

without permission

to be within

to spring out of the land

and/or sky

to originate

originally before everyone else

to belong but not belong

to be born from within

and conquered from without

to be indigent in your homelands

to be indignant about that

to have indigestion when

people call me Indigenous

when I just want to be

Sauk-Suiattle, Skagit, Chelan, Entiat, Wenatchee

Swan Dancers

when the swans get out to dance
everyone clears the floor
hush, hush, hush
their wings beat the earth
the drumbeat keeps company

        dancing feet
        beat, beat, swoosh
        swans swing and sway
        smiles all around
        swans turn their long necks
        this way and that.

        feathers shimmer, fringe whips air

        high step, high step
        step high round the circle
        fly high until, until
        the drumbeat sighs

     stillness, moonrise in a dark sky
     only then, only then, do
     Bernice and Adelaide alight
     on the dirt floor, to their chairs,
     return, giggling

Nch'i-Wana

I fell once head
like a lover's rush
sink away
oh, sun distant
stone brown river
me to stillness
loosed sodden
in the darkness
keeping time
an elder voice
oh, river damned
feed my people
river dammed
stop your motion
around the waist
river be free
to the forest
then a wave
I no longer control
swept to surface
toward sun
into my lungs
sun bows, light
what I heard in
life within

first in river
headfirst sink
from light
green blue dream
tumult compels
except my memory
escaping for life
I hear a rattle
conducting current
hums a dirge
mountain stream
salmon run red
walls cannot
pulled by moon
of earth
you, life blood
desert valley roots
came for me
my motion
carrying song
breath broke
I exhaled water
my knowing
river deep
live, river, live

PDX Urban Indian Life

urban Indian
grub Costco salmon, wild rice
close eyes dream of home

I once felt full of
salmon, berries, deer, wild roots
tasting loss staves me

call the children home
simmer milk and salmon to
nourish reclaim them

A Dream of Language

a distant horizon of motherland, no, an ocean
ferocious rising and falling
so much that solid earth still undulates

left behind in silt a rib cage, a hip, a femur,
a jawbone, a skull awaits beneath an avalanche of air

on prairie splayed under unremitting light
was light the one unknown
In the deep blue? I cannot say

I do not know the cadence of
language like an ancient flood
sounding of ocean waves

washing over green grass, a speaker pours
language like liquid over drought dry ground

in the crowded camp the dancer and the tree
a thousand brightly colored ribbons break free
prayers float atop an open sea

in emergent mud bones re-gather a whale breaches
nearby a buffalo backstrokes our relations coming home

come quickly, sister and brother, the ocean is rising
on land dried in the silence of language
now the ancestral tongue is alive in our mouths and our ears

together as of old and as of now
our footsteps fit together, words are our bridge

Photographer Edward Curtis' Subjects in Three Parts

One: The Women

Angeline princess,
Chief Seattle child
a dollar a pose, windfall

photogravure prints
marked on paper, my face
sepia toned

hanging the laundry
he spied the woman's beauty
no, i am busy

for a cigarette
she will pose fire on paper
makes a hole, she steps through

this dress smells, who wore it
last? Why not my own clothing?
I am not alone

chinook bride, famous
where be my husband, I know
war dead, travesty

on gallery wall
all eternity I stand
he's dead, here am I

Two: Chief Joseph

photogravure, copper plated
imagination more than life
discovered lenses, windowpane
render brown and gold, a knife
in the back; Chief Joseph's face
worn with age, shaped by pain
Oklahoma prison, empty space
his inner ear hears the eagle's call
to the camera he exposes
memory of ankles bound in chains

oh, my Wallowa, my dreams do turn
to our mountain lake, how I yearn
my people, once more to return
ancient paths to where fires burn

Three: 21ˢᵗ Century Indians

everyone has a camera now
everyone can take great shots
selfies, landscapes, powwows
our faces like our ancestors

everyone can take great shots
canyons, prairies, ocean shores
our faces like our ancestors
our smiles are all our own

canyons, prairies, ocean shores
babies' faces, lovers' eyes
our smiles are all our own
on social media for all to see

babies' faces, lovers' eyes
to dance under starry skies
on Facebook for all to see
every intimacy, Instagram to see

to dance under starry skies
we're 21ˢᵗ Century Indians
every intimacy, the world to see
we own our images, don't we

we're 21ˢᵗ Century Indians
our photos hang in galleries
we own our images, don't we
Curtis took we give away for free

our photos hang in galleries
lines in our faces tell stories
Curtis took. We give away for free
what would our ancestors say

lines in our faces tell stories
selfies, landscapes, powwows
what would our ancestors say
everyone has a camera now

Ancestor Gold

a vein of gold shimmers in sunlight
I am alive to potential, falling
from my horse into a field of spring flowers
I thought I saw a woman, though
it is only the draw of metal formed in quartz
enough to save myself, my children
leave Fort Simcoe, live
in the mountains, hidden
from wars America is starting
with all our relations

our village, our families, our homelands
now on my horse, the nugget hidden between my breasts
I will buy all we need, gather my children
find a place on the edge of Pahto's snowline, live

Etymology /əˈpäləjē/

apo

away

asunder

completely unread

logia logos

honorable but

not recorded in the record books

to speak in defense

my own defense

to be justified, unjustified

vindicated

a travesty

a plea for pardon

lingering regrets

Siskiyou Pass

snow weighed down the sky as your car slid off the road
fir trees, festooned as if for Christmas, blur in tear-filled eyes
your wife and three-year-old child snuggle in the backseat
you calculate silently how long before a warm car grows cold

this blizzard blown off the Pacific is fierce but
in the backseat your wife reads a story about a boy
who first gave names to animals, your daughter says zebra, giraffe
worry, your familiar, creases your brow, do you remember?

a plow, an answer to an unspoken prayer, appears
brushing snow off Siskiyou Pass, behind it a stranger
opens a car window and calls, Need a ride?
soon you and your family are tucked in his warm car
traveling toward a slumbering town

so long ago, still I remember

Where you folks going, the stranger asks
Home, you say. the stranger's eyes fill
with tears, as he says, I would be so happy
if I could see my son's child.

outside the moon wans in cloud breaks
ice blue stars burn cold
snoring bears beneath snow drifts, I remember

a motel owner woken from sleep, seems yet to dream
when he says, Madonna and baby must be kept warm
you take the keys while the radio crackles more snow
I'll get you a tow in the morning, that pass is no place
for travelers tonight, he turns back to bed

soon, we are too, to sleep, to dream and not remember

in the early morning you call your dad, We're safe from harm,
you half shout in a payphone. We'll be home waiting, the deep voice
of your dad intones, pies are baking, take your time, be safe

for the first time in a long time you think we'll be fine, remember

in morning's dim light this town treats strangers
like family, it's a holiday when everyone wants to
offer a helping hand, outside children wear homemade
tasseled hats, coats pulled tight by mittened hands
watching from our car window, I remember

finally, we arrive, a familiar tree filled with light
fire crackles behind, your wife says, Home is always now
and as long as we are together, we are far from harm

this happened many years ago, tonight a blizzard outside has me
remembering by my own fire, part of me remains the child
in that car feeling safe with my mom and dad, even now
we remain together in revere, still I remember

Jazz Parents

when they told me jazz was the pop music of their day, I knew I
was born at the wrong time

her favorite song "My Funny Valentine" could only be my mom's
song for my dad

my mother intoned your lips are laughable, un-

photo-

graphable

peeling laughter how words

fit

her voice formed by convent school choir practice

refined by a Tacoma

radio station coming in clear

she found

 her sing out

somewhere between the chirps

of Mildred Bailey

who trans-

fixed war dancers

in the black of Coeur d'Alene night

and

socialite dancers

dipping and whirling

squeaking and

scuffing on

the Waldorf dance-

floor

broadcast coast-to-coast

growl of Eartha Kitt

her unearthly rumble

Lady Bird couldn't stand

couldn't silence

don't turn off the trans-

istor

my mother issued forth a melodious Thelonious vocal

stream, a hint of Sassy, a hint of Dakota's

flirtatious purr

stay, little valentine, stay

oh, stay

my dad wants to be a cool cat in shades

utters not a word

just a vibe, catch it if you can

when her song ends, he stands transfixed

her death haunts him like a half-remembered song

until two decades

later

wracked with cancer

"A Broken-Hearted Melody" vibrated out of the tumor

ooh, ah, ooh, ah, ooh ah

embedded in mu-

tant cells that kill

in time, I'm keeping it real

alive

swinging

to my parent's jive

in my heart

Oscar Pettiford's

stomp dance

Sudden Death

an earlier generation   slid   under desks to hide   from unseen
threats

left initials carved in wooden desks   my fingers to trace

my 7-year-old mind   could count seconds $10-30-60$
seconds

to impact   at nearby Fairchild   Air Force Base

oblivion   in the mist   of my Catholic childhood   was
reason

for adherence   to rosaries and alms   always ready   for
certain death

like a mother   who stepped off a curb   to meet a
runaway bus

that carried her   to certain death   my expectation: high
likelihood

of nuclear   bomb   and if that wasn't   enough

further worries   of seeing the Virgin Mary   in the school
yard green

in first grade   I learned the Virgin   told Portuguese
children

the date   the world   would end

at Our Lady of Fatima   School   in Spokane, Washington

there was no   actual need   to tell me   because

I already knew   it would be   Wednesday   at noon when   air raid   sirens blared   city wide

I only   wondered   when it happened

would there be anyone   left to shut

the blasted thing off

Taking my Place

when I was young, the elder ones seemed to know everything
I followed them thinking I would follow them forever

now I am the one who must remember
the rituals that mark life and death
there are ones who follow me observing
can they see the uncertainty in my step

is memory enough to know where to place the plate
how to burn the sweet grass, remember distant linage
laugh to cover uncertainty
we laugh at how much we forget

I wonder if the elders felt this way too, struggling
to remember everything, laughing when memory slipped out of
reach

When First We Met

on the mantel stands the familiar
picture, you and I together
holding hands, outside snow and
night are falling together

let's shake dust from the quilt
I sewed from scrap
times of mourning are
in our past now we place
our shared memory
and photographs on the shelf

we have nowhere to go, light the
candles, turn up the stereo, we
slow dance as when first we met

we warm the soup
sauté the mushrooms we foraged
over conversation there will be
no moonrise tonight
only the hush of snow falling
on this good ground

falling to slumber, leaning on
each other, on this well-worn
couch, my head on your shoulder
your head on mine
as when first we met

Industrial River

River
Electric
Current
Ongoing
Generations
Nch'i Wána
Independence
Teardown
Inspires
Our Peoples
Now

Channel
Obscured
Local
Umbrage
Made
Barriers for
Indian fishers
An Affront

Annihilate
Nature:
Dams

Salmon
Nearly
Always
Knowingly
Escape

Return to
Independent
Visionary
Environmental
Reform
System

Linage
Ancient
Micro-predatory
Parasitic
Eel
Remember how
Yummy

Challenges
Happen
In journeys
Native
Oceanic
Open water
Kin

Salt and oil
Tenderize
Every morsel
Eaten
Late season
Harvest
Each year
Arrive hungry
Dear

Stayed
Titan
Under
Raging waters
Growing
Exponentially
Outer skeletal
Neanderthal era

Ostentatious
Rarified
Creatures
Applause

Engage
Now in
Demolition
And Stop
Nefarious
Greed
Extinction
Racing to
Early
Death

Special
Privileged
Encounter
Catalogued
In
Everyone's
Sacred memory

Time's up
Extricate
Appreciate
Revive by
Deconstructing
Operations
We
Never approved

Recognize
Every
Chance
Of
Verifying
Existence
Recovery
Yes, and more

Etymology | jen-uh-sahyd

geno – cide

ethnocide

race killing

intent: destruction

in whole or in part

a nation

a race

a religious people

a people of a faith

since the word was invented

in 1940

to make sense

of what cannot be made sense

use of the word

increased

one thousand percent

still reasons to use this word

grow daily

Declaring Our Indigene

a woman from Panama with a long think braid
greets me in the security line at the United Nations
she calls me sister, though we have never met
lingering, she tells me she has come before

in line there are many waiting
in their Indigene, their clothes, their hair
their hats, their words all speak of homes
where their struggles to survive, protect

lands, waters, forests, desert, permafrost
all beautiful in the earth and of the earth
even the children, most of all the children, who
will carry forward language and song we hope

the United Nations built in the sorrow
for six million deed, the word genocide
invented to represent unimaginable
horror against a people, the word invented

only to find no end to this word's use on this violent
earth, humanity displaying its worst
impulses Israeli hostages, the devastation of Gaza
a bitter taste today, an unwelcome reminder for

the survivors of over 100 million lost
in what is now called the Americas, we are
descended of the few who survived many
genocides, who resisted repeated extermination

in the café, European diplomats bum lights from
Native leaders with whom they have nothing
more in common than the smoke from cigarettes
maybe more communion than they've ever had

in that moment we did not know how long
it would take to pass a declaration still
our presence at the United Nations as food
cigarettes, even the toilet paper runs out

Bird Life

hummingbird side swipes
drooping lilies, alights fragile
stem grows skyward

eagle pair take flight
round dancing across the sky
distracting the earthbound

nuthatch flock
angel white wings flutter
making a tower in the air

blue plum yellow flesh
early dream, daydream, sweet burst
raven takes a bite

Passage

For David Spencer Sr.

David Spencer Sr. was a confessional poet who wrote in both English and the Northern Lushootseed language of his Tulalip Tribes. He was a self-taught poet inspired by the likes of Sylvia Plath and Anne Sexton. He was a speaker of his tribal language, raised by grandparents who were polyglot speakers of diverse dialects and languages rooted in the lands and waters of the Coast Salish Tribes and First Nations. The Coast Salish have continuously governed lands claimed by Canada and the United States on the shores of the Salish Sea, which stretches hundreds of miles from Olympia, Washington, to the north end of Vancouver Island in British Columbia between the Cascade and Olympic mountain ranges. Historically, the Coast Salish traded with nations to the east, to north, south, and across the Pacific Ocean. David, my husband's cousin, met on poetry for a long afternoon on June 30, 2023, in between his chemotherapy treatments. We shared a love for haiku. David said that writing haiku in the Lushootseed language was challenging because the words are many syllables long, including prefixes and suffixes. These long words can take up a whole haiku line by themselves. David wondered if we could write haiku according to our cultural traditions as Coast Salish people, such as using four lines to represent the sacred number for Tulalip, six to represent the number sacred to Sauk-Suiattle. Not long after David was hospitalized for the last time. I visited him in the hospital to read his beloved Sylvia Plath, her rhythm beating like a drum. Although he was semi-conscious at the time, his toe tapped in time with her rhythm. On the night he was dying, his family gathered in the hospital to wait. I returned home and decided to write some haiku-inspired poems in the way he suggested, varying the form. I have since learned that Japanese poets have experimented with different forms of haiku for more than a century.

words

october moon shines cold
as the poet dies wordlessly
his words pour out on lawn
pirouetting alone

gathering

for days the old ones
came to gab but could not say
words because poet
shedding skin, body
freed his tongue to tell
the truth for all time

shaker

a really good shake
toe tapping, rhythm
poet was a shaker from way
back to eternity

wordless

as a lad no word
he said, his grandpa wonders
what holds back poet's
song? black letters on a page

regrets

so many cloud po-
et's mind, worries very great
Sylvia Plath sad
still, poet writes on

family

donuts sliders blue
Gatorade family
await poet's death

heart song

poet said you are tech-
nical but do you know your own
heart song when it cries out

Sauk-Suiattle Struggles

This series describes some of the challenges faced by this federally recognized tribe that lives under the Glacier Peak volcano, on top of the lahar from an eruption around 1700, Sauk-Suiattle history recounts how boulders were thrown about in the volcanic explosion, landing on the banks of the Sauk River which shifts its course from year to year. Nearby the Oso mudslide of 2014, considered the deadliest in U.S. history. The Lushootseed word for landslide is the same word for vomit, signifying what the earth looks like when it has lost all cohesion. The stories of the tribe go back to before the Ice Age and the floods. Some of our history is buried under the lava flow. Some of our history is writ large in the Cascade Mountains.

who knows the map in our hearts
who draws the lines on round earth
on this curved swell of volcanic eschew
blanket of giant maple leaf, whisper of cedar
and fir, whose voice does challenge ocean wind
crashing into mountain face and curving estuary
who can find out?

I, a granddaughter of chief siyʔxʷaɬ, I am a biased correspondent
a juggler of foreign words, an asker of hard
questions, I will find out, grandfather

we are the saʔqʷəbixʷ and suyaƛʔbixʷ
some of us are one, some the other, some both
we are all related, born of related families
east and west of the Cascade Mountains
topped white with snow, to the rising mist on Sauk Prairie
to where the river called Skagit runs, to the lake
where the old chief lived, and everyone came to see him

place names in the enemy's language
West of the Cascade Mountains: Baker Lake, Birdsview, Cascade,
Marblemount, Concrete on the River called Skagit
the lake called Ross, at Conway way down river too
above Oso, Darrington, south to the Skykomish, to Sultan
East of the Cascade Mountains:
near Entiat, Lake Chelan, the river called Columbia
where Chief Jim Brown and Wewatikin
were born to their hereditary chief father and Sauk mother

our extended families' cedar plank houses were everywhere
our cabins were everywhere. our rock shelters were
on our seven paths across the Cascade Mountains
our crab apple gardens very old and still alive in these mountains
our fire rings still at our fish camps too, and
deep in the hearts of our people, our fires still burn

thirteen cedar plank houses on Sauk Prairie
five cedar plank houses up the Suiattle
a schoolhouse on the Suiattle
a big ceremonial house elsewhere
many more cedar plank houses
on either side of the river called Skagit
some homes, some ceremonial
at a place called miskaiwhu for prophet
there were many plank houses

the miskaiwhu has changed generationally
our prophecy continues
from time's beginning

at the national archive, they said you were no more
no they said there is no such thing as you

no, sauk, no suiattle, no hyphenation, no combination
no hybrid lineage of generations on this
pacific rim facing mountainside under northern lights
none, no existence, nowhere, no time, no breath

at the National Archives of the United States in Washington, D.C,
the clerk speaking with all authority amassed by empire said to me

 you do not exist

excuse me, sir, let me turn this well-constructed table for a moment
as I deal with your assumed certainty of this precariously
hung foundation over this Atlantic wetland
overlain with greenschist and shoe polish, a single faulty timber
may yet unhinge, topple empire, then who would stand

none other than the treaty signers
the nations you called no more

salmon catch in waterfall
hunting bear, elk, deer
gathering mountain goat hair
tending root gardens
planting crab apple orchards timed
to ripen when salmon spawn

we have right to our own languages
every tribe has its own ways of speaking, knowing

I fear this will be used against my people,
we are a confederacy of many chiefs
I fear this will be used against us

the matriarch said

at the state office, they couldn't find the email
despite much searching, couldn't see why this small tribe
given to the word NO need ever be asked, wished for plan
maybe they will go away, sent a spy to find
a young man to sacrifice for mine and extraction
when I raised complaint grasping up every magic of
this media age, the director said she didn't know, she
hung up the phone, shut up her ear, ended
electronic transmission
she ran as far as she could from this small tribe
from this mountainside
searching for how to get away

why don't you run for congress, miss director
that is, at least, a long way from here

Congressman Lloyd Meed sent a letter
delivered in 1971, it said
it is our belief at the US of A
that the Sauk-Suiattle Tribe
was signatory, signed and dotted
the treaty at Point Elliott
based on several facts
most important that Indian Claims Commission equated
the treaty name Sah-Ku-Meh(u)
with the present-day Sauk-Suiattle Indian Tribe

our answer was clear we signed the treaty
sending the subchief to sign when
Chief Wewatikin was leading the protocol of nations
as they landed their canoes and also Wewatikin
was busy delivering the mail
to all the tribes and all the federal officials present
because the chief's day job was mailman

in our long memory two important things happened on January
22, 1855
even if one of them was terrible and the other was necessary
the treaty was signed
and Wewatikin delivered the mail

the ancestor went before
ferreting out hidden text and footnote
pulling as if from air the buried
mention, all but forgotten under the crush of paper
we are but a small tribe, survivors of catastrophic
invasion of germs and captors, survivors of diaspora
flung like dandelion seeds world round and
round, we who once numbered in the thousands
who marked up this west slope of the ring of fire
with rock and tree, planted orchard and berry field
that thrive still even though they say no one planted these
no gardener no sculptor no intelligent life
to sing this language incorporated from bird song
to write the story of mountain ancestors in tree bark
to touch water that once touched earth's center

now our clean water falls out of mountainsides
crashing into valleys, no, there no one is here

Upriver Valleys Governed: Sauk, Suiattle, Cascade, Baker, White Chuck

and all the tributaries of the river called Skagit

Sauk-Suiattle censuses once counted 3000 citizens

U.S. Census in 1920 counted 17 (genocide by pandemic, genocide by poverty)

350 tribal citizens counted for in 2020

31 tribal citizens disenrolled in 2021 (self-induced genocide)

I report to the elders over lunch all I learned down below
then we listen for our ancestors' counsel in the chirp
of thrush language
our generations in diaspora have lost sight of our shared song
wrung from this volcanic soil, birthed of earthen fire
we dug our own divides using daggers
of lie and tv rerun legend, delete our hyphenated
family name, delete the hyphen that connects us
we point fingers, wage a war of the vicious
variety that can only smell of family
with one reedy voice the ancestors cry
we are one people, many cousins seated in one canoe
clinging to the rim of a snow-covered sleeping volcano
our canoe will sink beneath the flood if we fail to hold
if we point fingers, we can't hold even our paddles
the weight of flood waters can crush us
but it hasn't yet, not under worse
circumstances than now beset us
put away your angry cry
put down the meth pipe
throw away the needle
drop your dagger
fire the lawyers who have gold nuggets for eyes

we are mountain goats scaling this cliff
searching rock face together
for life giving water drip and salt crystals
together

Dance Backwards
Individual
Another
Systemic
Policy
Obviously
Rancid
Approach

Rush of Wings
Endurance
Turbulent
Under
Radar
Never Fear

Home is Always Home
Our Tribes Are Calling Us Home
Moving Toward, Running into Open Arms
Enough, at Last, We Are Enough

Celilo

dos-wail-opsh

chush

wynoochee

multnomah   hi hi kwitht

loowit   koosah

elwha   sol duc   tumwata   sauk

wah gwin   chamokane   taitnab

kwyayish   lill li whop   dos-wail-opsh

san ate koo   hamma hamma

snoqualmie   hoko   klickitat

pa-luš-sa   stluputqu

canyon echo   mist sings   sacred roar

what remains alive

what may never be again

ACKNOWLEDGMENTS

"Acknowledgement Two" was published in Poetry Northwest, Fall 2024

"Desloot's Wápaas" was published in Voices of the River, published by the Confluence Project, October 2024

NOTES

Regarding tribal languages: I am descended from tribes on both sides of the North Cascade Mountain Range Words in the Yakama Ichishikín Sínwit and words in Lushootseed, the language of Sauk-Suiattle and related tribes, reference from The Lushootseed Dictionary and Sauk-Suiattle documents.

Definitions from the Sauk-Suiattle Indian Tribe and The Lushootseed Dictionary:

   haboo – story, myth

   miskaiwhu – prophet

Definitions from the Ichishikín Sínwit Yakama/Yakima Sahaptin Dictionary:

   wápaas – a small, twined basket, used when picking berries or digging roots

   Nch'i wána – the Columbia River

The poem "Remember Celilo" uses the names of waterfalls from across the Northwest in a variety of tribal languages from across the Northwest. The list is not all inclusive, but rather a sample of publicly available tribal names for waterfalls that were written in the English alphabet. The intention is that English speakers can sound out these words and feel the flow of Indigenous languages in their mouths and perhaps get a sense of what these language mean to us, as well to sense the sacredness of our waterfalls.

"By the Creekside" is a poem written in homage to poet Carolyn Kizer poem and in correction to her poem "By the Riverside" which was published 1961. Kizer's poem mistakenly refers to two thieves who were hung. This is what actually happened. Near the end of the Yakama War (1855–1858) the Yakama war chief Owhi went to U.S. Army Col. George Wright's camp near present day Spokane, Wash., by a creek, to negotiate peace. Instead, Wright ordered Owhi to be held captive, while confined in irons. Soon his son Qualchan came to the camp looking for his father. Wright immediately ordered Qualchan hung and later ordered the desecration of Qualchan's body. Owhi was shot while trying to escape. These were not thieves as Kizer's poem stated, but rather Owhi was a political prisoner and Qualchan was unjustly executed. The creek where this occurred was known for more than century as Hangman Creek, its name was changed in the 1990s to Latah Creek, though the name is still used in nearby Idaho. Kizer unwittingly repeated a false narrative that had circulated since the Yakama War, still as efforts to tell this history occur and racist placenames are changed to tribal language name, this poem intends to posthumously gently correct an important American poet.

The "Etymology" series is documentary poetry that is based upon the etymologies of words that are commonly used in U.S.-Tribal Government relations. There is also imagery based upon the etymologies in these poems.

The poem "Acknowledgement One" refers to legal information provided to public officials that say tribal acknowledgements have no legal standing. Some of the images are based upon the journals of U.S. soldiers who fought in the wars against tribes in the Northwest.

"Acknowledgement Two" is loosely based upon oral history of my uncle Alvin Settler (1930-2008), a Yakama tribal fisher and Chief Judge of the Yakama Nation. When he was dying, my uncle asked me to conduct formal oral, recorded histories with him. The conclusions in the poem are my own, and the context of the poem also includes other tribal treaty fishers in the Mid-Columbia River.

"Acknowledgement Three" is based upon conversations I had with her grandmother Ermina Goudy Edsall (1911-1991). In this poem underline sections with nothing written above it are meant to symbolize information that is lost or forgotten as a result of boarding schools. It also symbolizes silence or no response from the United States.

"Acknowledgement Four" is based upon the oral history provided by Sauk-Suiattle Chair Norma Joseph (1947-2023) concerning actions of the U.S. Forest Service in the 1960s against Sauk-Suiattle allotment holders, specifically focused upon the burning of Chief Leo Brown's home without notice. Chief Brown was Chair Joseph's grandfather, and my great-great uncle. In this poem underline sections are used to show the lack of response from federal agencies. Tribally Norma Joseph is my aunt, though in a Euro-American family tree we would be cousins.

"The Mountains, Our Ancestors" is based upon a story and details were provided by Norma Joseph that she learned from her grandfather Chief Leo Brown. The names of the mountains in Lushootseed were provided by Norma Joseph.

"Desloot's Wápaas" was written after a genealogical researcher among the Northwest Tribes gave me the name of my great-great grandmother on the Wenatchi side of my family, Desloot.

"Sauk-Suiattle Struggles" is a poem that is based upon an extended conversation I had with Norma Joseph over several years, as she taught me Sauk-Suiattle culture, lands and language. The poem references Sauk Chief Jim Brown, siyʔxʷał, who is my great-great grandfather, and his brother who preceded him as hereditary chief, Wewatikin. The opinions in the poem are my own.

Many poems in this collection are haiku-inspired and haibun-inspired. These are written in respect for these Japanese forms of poetry.

ABOUT THE AUTHOR

Kara Briggs is a writer and a poet who lives on the Tulalip Reservation in Washington state. She is Sauk-Suiattle tribal citizen and a direct descendant of Yakama Nation. She is also descended Irish and English, and as an undergraduate studied abroad in Dublin, Ireland, with the leading Irish poets of the time.

In 2024 she completed her Master of Fine Arts at the Institute of American Indian Arts, where she studied with Navajo poet Esther Belin, with Oglala poet Layli Longsoldier, with Mvskoke poet Jennifer Elise Foerster. She previously graduated from The Evergreen State College with a Master of Public/Tribal Administration. Her bachelor's degree in English is from Whitworth College, in Spokane, her hometown.

She is a career writer, having spent two decades as a journalist, including at *The Oregonian* in Portland, *The Spokesman-Review* in Spokane, Wash., and *ICT* (formerly *Indian Country Today*). She has also worked in higher education, in public affairs, and now is Vice President for Tribal Lands and Waters Stewardship at Ecotrust, supervising teams that support environmental work with tribes across the West Coast of the United States.

She is past president of the Native American Journalists Association and the Center for Women and Democracy. Her poetry reflects the places she has lived in the Intermountain West, in the historic temperate rainforest land of Western Oregon and Western Washington, all a stone's throw from the Canadian border; now she and her husband live on an allotment, issued to her husband's grandfather under the Point Elliott Treaty, in a forest near the Salish Sea, between Seattle and Vancouver, B.C.

www.ingramcontent.com/pod-product-compliance
Lightning Source LLC
Chambersburg PA
CBHW052211120625
28167CB00021B/318